Forty Days
FAST

Cultivating a Heart for God

Pana Mamea

ISBN 978-1-64300-743-4 (Paperback)
ISBN 978-1-64300-744-1 (Digital)

Covenant Books, Inc.
11661 Hwy 707
Murrells Inlet, SC 29576
www.covenantbooks.com

CONTENTS

INTRODUCTION

F orty Days has great significance in the way God works in the life of a follower of Jesus Christ. Throughout the Old and New Testaments, forty days represented change, transition, time of renewal or new beginning. God often used forty days to prepare nations, cities, and individuals for the next level of their purpose in the Lord. Consider these biblical examples:

- Noah (Gen. 7:4)—forty days and nights of rain destroyed unrestrained wickedness on earth and paved the way for the ultimate revelation of the Savior of the world.
- Moses (Exod. 16:35)—forty days and nights on Mt. Sinai in the presence of God revealed the standard of God and the depravity of man.
- Twelve Spies (Num. 13:25)—forty days and nights of spying out Canaan revealed the beauty of the promised land and the refusal of the majority to believe God's Word.
- Israel (1 Sam. 17:16)—forty day and nights Goliath challenged the nation of Israel and was summarily defeated by David, and victory was secured for Israel.
- Nineveh (Jon. 3:4)—forty days Jonah preached judgment against Nineveh, which precipitated repentance and the mercy of God.
- Jesus (Matt. 4:2)—forty days and nights of fasting and being tempted by the devil brought about victory over temptation and the unleashing of Jesus's ministry.

As you embark on this forty-day journey, you too will encounter a change in heart, a transition to the next stage of your purpose, and a renewal of your passion for God. According to the Talmud (Jewish law), it takes forty days for an embryo to be formed in its mother's womb. I believe these next forty days will in like manner cultivate a heart for God, a heart for the things of God, a heart for the people of God, and a heart for those who know not God. Get ready to be rebuked, renewed, and released into the fullness of God's grace for your life. Have fun and enjoy the transformation.

1 Samuel 5:1–5

Then the Philistines took the ark of God and brought it from Ebenezer to Ashdod. When the Philistines took the ark of God, they brought it into the house of Dagon and set it by Dagon. And when the people of Ashdod arose early in the morning, there was Dagon, fallen on its face to the earth before the ark of the Lord. So they took Dagon and set it in its place again. And when they arose early the next morning, there was Dagon, fallen on its face to the ground before the ark of the Lord. The head of Dagon and both the palms of its hands were broken off on the threshold; only Dagon's torso was left of it. Therefore neither the priests of Dagon nor any who come into Dagon's house tread on the threshold of Dagon in Ashdod to this day.

HE WILL SET YOUR HOUSE IN ORDER

G ood day, Saints!

The Philistines took the Ark of God, which represents the presence of God, to Ashdod and set it in the House of Dagon, their local deity. When the people of Ashdod arose early in the morning, Dagon was prostrate facedown before the Ark of the Lord (1 Sam. 5:1–5). On this dreadful day, the Philistines discovered the truth about their god. In the presence of the God of heaven, Dagon was exposed as a usurper, imposter, and a lie. He was unable to defend himself let alone the people who placed their trust in him. The presence of God in their midst revealed their utter need of a Savior.

How many counterfeits are currently taking up residence in our heart? Interrupt the mundane with the invitation of the presence of God. He will rearrange the furniture in order to maximize life, expose the trespasser, and give him an eviction notice. In the presence of the Holy Spirit there is freedom. Let Him come into your heart and set your house in order.

Prayer

Dear God, come into my heart and rearrange the furniture of my life. Expose the trespassers and issue an eviction notice. Set my house in order and maximize the effectiveness of my life that I may bring glory and honor to Your name. In Jesus's name I pray, amen.

DAY 2

Proverbs 18:10

The name of the Lord is a strong tower;
The righteous run to it and are safe.

TAKE THE HIGH GROUND

Good day, Saints!

Proverbs 18 verse 10 reminds us, "The name of the Lord is a strong tower, and the righteous run into it and are safe." A literal Hebrew translation of the text doesn't emphasize safety as much as it does perspective: "A tower of strength is the name of Jehovah, into it the righteous runs, and is set on high." In times of war, having a strategic vantage point oftentimes can determine life or death. Taking the high ground—in other words, running into a strong tower—would expedite victory. Jesus is our high ground! From His viewpoint, all our battles will be won. No weapon formed against us will prosper, nor any barrier fixed before us be impenetrable when we are standing on the high ground!

Take the high ground and go to war. Clucking with turkeys will prevent you from soaring like an eagle. Reject fear's invitation to envelop your soul. Run to Jesus and let His perspective simplify your response to the devil's harassing accusations. His presence provides the power, protection, and perspective we need to complete our assignment. Take the high ground!

Prayer

Dear God, you are my strong tower, and I relinquish my trust in my limited perspective and make a fresh commitment to run unto You to ensure assignment completion. Elevate my eyes so I can see from Your perspective. In Jesus's name, amen.

2 Peter 3:9

The Lord is not slack concerning *His* promise, as some count slackness, but is longsuffering toward us, not willing that any should perish but that all should come to repentance.

Psalm 145:8

The Lord *is* gracious and full of compassion, Slow to anger and great in mercy.

Romans 2:4

Or do you despise the riches of His goodness, forbearance, and longsuffering, not knowing that the goodness of God leads you to repentance?

SLOW TO ANGER AND RICH IN LOVE

Good day, Saints!

Once again, God reveals His abundant mercy by prolonging the revelation of His judgment. The apostle Peter gives us insight into a side of God that has been shielded from our eyes, because it will only happen once. Throughout history, glimpses of God's anger have been witnessed by some, but on the day of the Lord, all of heaven, earth, and those under the earth will see the full unleashing of the wrath of

God against those unwilling to take shelter in His Son Jesus Christ. Pockets of disaster, economic upheaval, and political instability serve as signposts warning us to flee into the loving arms of God. The Lord is merciful and compassionate, slow to get angry, and filled with unfailing love. Seek the Lord while He is revealing Himself as a benevolent King, before He is forced to put on His judgment garb.

God longs for mankind to commune with Him out of an overflow of gratitude for His kindness. It's God's kindness that leads us to repentance. But more often than not, negligence, rejection, and idolatry characterize our responses. He remains patient, not wishing that any should perish but that all should reach repentance. Let His love overwhelm us before His judgment undercuts us.

Prayer

Dear God, thank you for Your loving patience with me. My mind often forgets the many storms You have brought me through, and my heart so easily wanders from Your presence when I am seduced by a calm. Help me to fully appreciate Your longsuffering, that I may truly enjoy Your amazing grace. In Jesus's name, amen.

Nehemiah 7:35

The sons of Bakbuk,
the sons of Hakupha,
the sons of Harhur,

1 Corinthians 15:58

Therefore, my beloved brethren, be steadfast, immovable, always abounding in the work of the Lord, knowing that your labor is not in vain in the Lord.

Ezekiel 22:30

So I sought for a man among them who would make a wall, and stand in the gap before Me on behalf of the land, that I should not destroy it; but I found no one.

HEAVEN KNOWS YOUR NAME

Good day, Saints!

Who are Bakbuk, Hakupha, and Harhur? Most Christians, let alone the general public, have never heard of these individuals; but their contribution to the rebuilding of the wall of Jerusalem helped to facilitate the revival of a city. In the book of Nehemiah chapter 7, the author lists all the names of the families who were responsible for the complete restoration of the city wall. Under harsh criticism and threats of violence, these brave warriors labored sacrificially without complaint. Their unswerving focus and faith in God enabled them to complete the wall of protection for the city in only fifty-two days and began the process of reestablishing the right relationship with God. The work of these unknown servants may go unnoticed by the majority, but their obedience is forever etched on God's heart.

Your labor for the Lord is not in vain. All the little things you do for God that oftentimes go unnoticed by the masses are faithfully being recorded in heaven. The godly perseverance of the saints in prayer and godliness, especially in difficult seasons, provides a wall of protection for family and city. In Ezekiel 22:30, God went looking among men to see who would build up the wall and stand before Him in the gap on behalf of the land so He wouldn't have to destroy it, but He found none. Don't let your generation be found faithless! Stand in the gap! Put on your armor! Heaven knows your name!

Prayer

Dear God, thank you for being mindful of me. Sometimes I feel like I am going so fast and yet making no progress. Help me to remain diligent regardless of the outward appearance, knowing that You are watching over me. In Jesus's name, amen.

Romans 8:28

And we know that all things work together for good to those who love God, to those who are the called according to *His* purpose.

1 Thessalonians 5:16

Rejoice always.

Philippians 1:6

Being confident of this very thing, that He who has begun a good work in you will complete *it* until the day of Jesus Christ.

Isaiah 54:17

No weapon formed against you shall prosper,
And every tongue *which* rises against you in judgment
You shall condemn.
This *is* the heritage of the servants of the LORD,
AND THEIR RIGHTEOUSNESS *is* from Me," Says the LORD.

Philippians 4:4

Rejoice in the Lord always. Again I will say, rejoice!

REJOICE FOREVERMORE

Good day, Saints!

Trouble. Persecution. Fear. Doubt. Sorrow. Worry. Discouragement. Grace. Hope. Faith. Love. Light. They were his favorite. All throughout the region, Paul joyously mentions the glowing example of the Thessalonian church. Against daunting opposition, they remained steadfast in their love for Jesus Christ. It was a witness that revealed the depth of faith in the sovereignty of the Almighty God. A recognition that "all things work together for good to those that love God and are called according to His purpose." An understanding that God is in control regardless of the circumstances. A resolution to rejoice forevermore because the best and worst of the earth will pale significantly in comparison to the joy of heaven.

When the external state of things doesn't coincide with internal belief, rejoice! When vision is clouded by thundering storms, rejoice! If confusion threatens to circumvent peace, rejoice! He who began a good work in you is faithful to complete it. No weapon formed against you shall prosper. Rejoice in the Lord always. Again, I say rejoice!

Prayer

Dear God, I rejoice in you. No amount of earthly discouragement will ever silence my trust in You. You are sovereign, and I know my life is safe in Your hands. Your praises shall always be on my lips. In Jesus's name, amen.

Ephesians 5:15–16

See then that you walk circumspectly, not as fools but as wise, redeeming the time, because the days are evil.

Ephesians 5:1–14

Therefore be imitators of God as dear children. And walk in love, as Christ also has loved us and given Himself for us, an offering and a sacrifice to God for a sweet-smelling aroma.

But fornication and all uncleanness or covetousness, let it not even be named among you, as is fitting for saints; neither filthiness, nor foolish talking, nor coarse jesting, which are not fitting, but rather giving of thanks. For this you know, that no fornicator, unclean person, nor covetous man, who is an idolater, has any inheritance in the kingdom of Christ and God. Let no one deceive you with empty words, for because of these things the wrath of God comes upon the sons of disobedience. Therefore do not be partakers with them.

For you were once darkness, but now *you are* light in the Lord. Walk as children of light (for the fruit of the Spirit *is* in all goodness, righteousness, and truth), finding out what is acceptable to the Lord. And have no fellowship with the unfruitful works of darkness, but rather expose *them*. For it is shameful even to speak of those things which are done by them in secret. But all things that are exposed are made manifest by the light, for whatever makes manifest is light. Therefore He says: "Awake, you who sleep, Arise from the dead, And Christ will give you light."

Genesis 18:32

Then he said, "Let not the Lord be angry, and I will speak but once more: Suppose ten should be found there?"

And He said, "I will not destroy *it* for the sake of ten."

IS YOUR LIGHT SHINING?

Good day, Saints!

Samuel Adams, at the signing of the Declaration of Independence in 1776, stated, "Neither the wisest constitution nor the wisest laws will secure the liberty and happiness of a people whose manners are universally corrupt." In a similar temper, the apostle Paul exhorts the Ephesian church, saying, "Be careful how you walk, not as unwise men but wise making the most of your time, because the days are evil" (Eph. 5:15–16). Gratitude is best expressed through obedience. Indifference is the response of a heart that has forgotten the love and sacrifice Christ has made on his/her behalf. Evil desires to darken our minds and heart, but the best defense against a foreboding darkness is a bright shining life illuminated by the love of God (Eph. 5:1–14).

An increase of darkness must be confronted by an increase of light. No amount of legislation can dispel evil if individual citizens are operating in the dark. God searched for ten upright persons in order to avert the destruction of Sodom, but ten could not be found

(Gen. 18:32). Refuse to allow the shadows of evil to dim your light. Raise your banner high and let your light shine bright so the world can be saved.

Prayer

Dear God, make my life a candle that burns brightly with Your love and grace. Remove the blind spots in my heart that threaten to overshadow that light so those around me can find hope in You. In Jesus's name, amen.

DAY 7

Ephesians 5:13

But all things that are exposed are made manifest by the light, for whatever makes manifest is light.

THERE IS HEALING IN THE LIGHT

Good day, Saints!

"But all things become visible when they are exposed by the light, for everything that becomes visible is light" (Eph. 5:13). Paul's exhortation to the Ephesian church begins with a brief reminder of their dark past. It was a past riddled with images of evil deeds done in darkness that left many suffering alone in secret. Its effects produced alienation from God and disillusionment about self. However, its power to blind and banish the human heart was no match for the light of Jesus Christ. His light disarmed the power of darkness and restored God's original design. What the devil meant for evil now stands as a shining example of God's mercy and grace.

There is healing in the light. Deep darkness, private pain, and secret suffering are no match for the healing light of God's love. Wake up, you who are trapped in the doldrums of depression, and Christ will shine His light on you and disperse the darkness.

Prayer

Dear God, thank you for disarming the power of darkness in my life and shining Your healing light on my heart. Restore Your original design for me, and let it begin redefining my destiny. Burn away all of the clutter and make my heart Your home. In the name of your son Jesus Christ, amen.

DAY 8

> Blessed *be* the God and Father of our Lord Jesus Christ, who has blessed us with every spiritual blessing in the heavenly *places* in Christ

THE BLESSING OF HEAVEN IS WAITING

Good day, Saints!

"Blessed be the God and Father of our Lord Jesus Christ, who has blessed us with every spiritual blessing in heavenly places in Christ Jesus" (Eph. 1:3). Shouts of praise ring loudly throughout the land because the Father has elevated humanity above the animals. Through Christ our spirit man is brought back to life, and reconciliation with God is made possible. A clean heart, purified mind, and a clean conscience are available. Forgiveness of sin, deliverance from fear, and healing of diseases are accessible. We no longer have to be enslaved by the cravings and limitations of the flesh because in Christ Jesus we can stand boldly before the throne of grace in order to find mercy for every challenge we will face.

All the resources of heaven are on standby, waiting to be unleashed on your behalf. Living life according to our human instincts makes us no better than the animals. Through Jesus Christ, life will take on heavenly significance. Get out of the rat race so you can start living the life God destined for you to live. Look up! The blessings of heaven are waiting.

Prayer

Dear God, thank you for making the blessings of heaven accessible through Jesus Christ Your Son. Take me out of the unending cycle of meaninglessness and let heaven's plan for my life begin. Make me a vessel useful for Your kingdom. In Jesus's name, amen.

I have been crucified with Christ; it is no longer I who live, but Christ lives in me; and the *life* which I now live in the flesh I live by faith in the Son of God, who loved me and gave Himself for me. I do not set aside the grace of God; for if righteousness *comes* through the law, then Christ died in vain.

DO NOT NEGLECT SUCH A GREAT SALVATION

G ood day, Saints!

Paul rails against the hypocrisy of Peter, Barnabas, and other Jewish believers saying, "I have been crucified with Christ. It is no longer I who live, but Christ lives in me, and the life I now live in the flesh I live in the Son of God, who loved me and gave Himself for me." Continuing on, he says, "I do not set aside the grace of God, for if righteousness comes through the law, then Christ died in vain" (Gal. 2:20–21). Cultural norms were beginning to cloud the discernment of church leaders and the apostle Paul was not going to tolerate it for one second. On the surface, it seemed harmless, but its inevitable outcome would be the accentuation of human effort and the minimizing of the person of Jesus Christ. A small "Jesus" gives way to a man-made salvation, which is no salvation at all. Jesus is God. He is second to none. He is our salvation alone. We are not justified by works of the law but by faith in Jesus Christ.

The prince of the power of the air is scheming day and night to create craftier ways to undeify Jesus Christ in the eyes of man. Since his interaction with Eve in the garden of Eden, his methods have changed little, but his message remains the same. His goal is to deify human effort and do away with dependence on God. Rekindle your devotion to Jesus Christ. Silence the voice of cultural relevance and lean wholeheartedly on Christ. Jesus as the author and finisher of our faith, so let us not neglect so great a salvation!

Prayer

Dear God, thank you for the sure foundation of Jesus Christ. Free me from the tendency of becoming self-righteous and hide me in Your love which casts out all fear. In Jesus's name, amen!

Galatians 1:8

But even if we, or an angel from heaven, preach any other gospel to you than what we have preached to you, let him be accursed.

Galatians 1:6–7

I marvel that you are turning away so soon from Him who called you in the grace of Christ, to a different gospel, which is not another; but there are some who trouble you and want to pervert the gospel of Christ.

John 14:6

Jesus said to him, "I am the way, the truth, and the life. No one comes to the Father except through Me."

EMBRACE THE CROSS

Good day, Saints!

They were zealous, passionate, and sincere, but they were sincerely wrong. The church in Galatia was under their theological barrage. Sadly, many succumbed to the lie. In a fatherly rage to protect this innocent body of believers, the apostle Paul exhorted the church saying, "Even if we or an angel from heaven should preach a gospel other than the one we preached to you, let him be eternally condemned" (Gal. 1:8). Anyone attempting to diminish the redemptive work of Christ on the cross by adding to it the need for human effort, or dismissing the deity of Christ by relegating Him to superhuman status, is perverting the gospel of Jesus Christ (Gal. 1:6–7).

Jesus declared to His disciples in John 14:6, "I am the way, the truth, and the life. No one comes to the Father except through me." A plethora of voices are vying for our attention. Its aim is to blind our eyes to the truth of Jesus Christ. A slight miscalculation in our understanding of the free gift of salvation that was made possible through the shed blood of Jesus Christ on the cross can result in a lifetime and eternity of regret. Purge the gospel of all man-made excesses and cling completely to Jesus. Embracing His cross secures our crown.

Prayer

Dear God, thank you for the redemptive work of Christ on the cross, which has made it possible for me to stand boldly in Your presence. Help me to never lose sight of the price You paid to ensure my freedom. In Jesus's name, amen!

Luke 8:43–48

Now a woman, having a flow of blood for twelve years, who had spent all her livelihood on physicians and could not be healed by any, came from behind and touched the border of His garment. And immediately her flow of blood stopped.

And Jesus said, "Who touched Me?"

When all denied it, Peter and those with him said, "Master, the multitudes throng and press You, and You say, 'Who touched Me?'"

But Jesus said, "Somebody touched Me, for I perceived power going out from Me." Now when the woman saw that she was not hidden, she came trembling; and falling down before Him, she declared to Him in the presence of all the people the reason she had touched Him and how she was healed immediately.

And He said to her, "Daughter, be of good cheer; your faith has made you well. Go in peace."

2 Corinthians 12:9

And He said to me, "My grace is sufficient for you, for My strength is made perfect in weakness." Therefore most gladly I will rather boast in my infirmities, that the power of Christ may rest upon me.

AT MY WEAKEST, HE BECAME MY STRENGTH

Good day, Saints!

Another broken dream. The doctors were so sure, but now I am broke. My condition forbids me to live a normal life. Anyone I touch or touches me will be deemed "unclean." Is isolation, rejection, and darkness all I have to look forward to? No! I will not be relegated to a life of despair. If I can just touch the hem of His garment, I will be healed. I am healed! I am healed! I am healed! (Luke 8:43–48).

Jesus, speaking to the apostle Paul during a time of confusion and despair in Paul's life said, "My grace is sufficient for you, for my strength is made perfect in weakness." When circumstances beyond our control begin tearing at the fabric of our security and we are utterly powerless to affect any change, look to Jesus Christ. He is the author and finisher of our destiny. Our strength in times of weakness. Our provider in times of need.

Prayer

Dear God, thank you for being my strength when I am weak. Help me to lean wholeheartedly on You during the good and bad times of life. In You I am safe, secure, and focused. In Jesus's name, amen.

2 Corinthians 4:8–10

We are hard-pressed on every side, yet not crushed; *we are* perplexed, but not in despair; persecuted, but not forsaken; struck down, but not destroyed—always carrying about in the body the dying of the Lord Jesus, that the life of Jesus also may be manifested in our body.

REVEALING JESUS

Good day, Saints!

"We are hard pressed on every side, but not crushed, perplexed, but not abandoned, struck down, but not destroyed. We always carry around in our body the death of Jesus, so that the life of Jesus may also be revealed in our body" (2 Cor. 4:8–10). The apostle Paul understood all too well that the hurts we live through today will shape our character for life. There is no other way. Jesus demonstrated that the best way to fulfill the purposes of God is to obey the will of the Father even when He seems distant. Through those dark seasons, a greater revelation of the life of Jesus will become apparent to all. It will also shine as a beacon of hope for those who are traveling with you.

Job already had an upright character, but through his struggles, we observe how an upright person behaves in the midst of tragedy. We have been given the awesome responsibility of shining the light of Christ to the world. The obstacles we endure may momentarily overshadow our perspective on God's promises, but take heart—in just a little while, and when you least expect it, God will give you a heavenly peek of the masterpiece your life is becoming. That view will provide a source of strength for today and inspire hope for tomorrow.

Prayer

Dear God, thank you for the trials and tribulation You have brought me through. Give me the proper perspective of Your sovereignty that I may be still even in the thick of the storm. In Jesus's name, amen.

DAY 13

2 Corinthians 3:7–18

Now if the ministry that brought death, which was engraved in letters on stone, came with glory, so that the Israelites could not look steadily at the face of Moses because of its glory, transitory though it was, will not the ministry of the Spirit be even more glorious? If the ministry that brought condemnation was glorious, how much more glorious is the ministry that brings righteousness! For what was glorious has no glory now in comparison with the surpassing glory. And if what was transitory came with glory, how much greater is the glory of that which lasts!

Therefore, since we have such a hope, we are very bold. We are not like Moses, who would put a veil over his face to prevent the Israelites from seeing the end of what was passing away. But their minds were made dull, for to this day the same veil remains when the old covenant is read. It has not been removed, because only in Christ is it taken away. Even to this day when Moses is read, a veil covers their hearts. But whenever anyone turns to the Lord, the veil is taken away. Now the Lord is the Spirit, and where the Spirit of the Lord is, there is freedom. And we all, who with unveiled faces contemplate the Lord's glory, are being transformed into his image with ever-increasing glory, which comes from the Lord, who is the Spirit.

HIS GLORY FOR MY GLORY

Good day, Saints!

As Moses descended from his encounter with God, he had to place a veil over his face to shield the people of God from the reflection of the glory of God shining on him. Over time, the glory faded. The ministry of the law had a glory, but the ministry of righteousness exceeds in much more glory. A veil remains over the minds and hearts of those attempting to prove their worth through good deeds. They bask in a short-lived glory. However, when a person turns to the Lord, the veil is taken away. The Lord is the Spirit and where the Spirit of the Lord is, there is liberty. But we all with unveiled face, beholding as in a mirror the glory of the Lord, are being transformed into the same image from glory to glory, just as by the Spirit of the Lord (2 Cor. 3:7–18).

The fading glory of good deeds can never satisfy like the glorious presence of the Holy Spirit when he is allowed to take residence in our heart. Through Him we have an unending communion with the King of glory. In His presence, we discover the true meaning of freedom and are transformed daily into the likeness of Jesus our glorious King. Embrace Jesus so your veil can be removed. Embrace Jesus so His glory can shine through you.

Prayer

Dear God, thank you for Your glory that does not fade with the passing of time. I cast aside my dimming glow and fully embrace your redemptive glory. Deliver me from self-righteousness and enable me to rest in your shine. In Jesus's name, amen.

1 Corinthians 5:5–6

Deliver such a one to Satan for the destruction of the flesh, that his spirit may be saved in the day of the Lord Jesus.

Your glorying *is* not good. Do you not know that a little leaven leavens the whole lump?

2 Corinthians 2:10–11

Now whom you forgive anything, I also *forgive.* For if indeed I have forgiven anything, I have forgiven that one for your sakes in the presence of Christ, lest Satan should take advantage of us; for we are not ignorant of his devices.

THE SATANIC SEDUCTION: UNREPENTANCE AND UNFORGIVENESS

Good day, Saints!

As long as he was unrepentant, Satan was unconcerned with his church attendance. The Corinthian church saw it as an extension of grace, but the apostle Paul recognized it as a satanic seduction. His rebuke was clear: "Hand this man over to Satan, so that his sinful nature may be destroyed and his spirit saved on the day of the Lord. Your boasting is not good. Don't you know that a little yeast works through the whole lump of dough?" (1 Cor. 5:5–6). Their obedience was immediate and commendable, but in their zeal for purity, they overlooked their responsibility to forgive. Satan was content with repentance as long as he remained disconnected from the church. Once again the apostle Paul realized that a satanic seduction was in operation and quickly instructed the church to forgive the repentant offender and restore him to the fold so that Satan doesn't outsmart us by defaming the holiness and grace of God. We are not ignorant of his schemes (2 Cor. 2:10–11).

An unrepentant church is a tool Satan uses to attack the justice and holiness of God. An unforgiving church is a tool Satan uses to tear down the love and grace of God. We must not be ignorant of his plans. Expose the satanic seduction! Let it begin with us. Are we harboring secret sins? Repent! Are we a haven of rest for the repentant sinner? If not, repent!

Prayer

Dear God, thank you that I am not ignorant of the devil's schemes. Help me to have a repentant heart so sin doesn't have a hold on me. Soften my heart so I can forgive those who have harmed me. In Jesus's name, amen.

John 3:16

For God so loved the world that He gave His only begotten Son, that whoever believes in Him should not perish but have everlasting life.

Romans 10:9–10

That if you confess with your mouth the Lord Jesus and believe in your heart that God has raised Him from the dead, you will be saved. For with the heart one believes unto righteousness, and with the mouth confession is made unto salvation.

Hebrews 10:26–27

For if we sin willfully after we have received the knowledge of the truth, there no longer remains a sacrifice for sins, but a certain fearful expectation of judgment, and fiery indignation which will devour the adversaries.

Romans 6:23

For the wages of sin *is* death, but the gift of God *is* eternal life in Christ Jesus our Lord.

STOP PAYING FOR YOUR OWN SINS

Good day, Saints!

Justice demands that every sin be punished. God's love compelled Him to pay for the sins of the world by placing their punishment on His Son Jesus Christ (John 3:16). Having satisfied His justice, God freely offers a pardon to all who would accept the payment Christ made on their behalf (Rom. 10:9–10). No one has to pay for their own sin, yet multitudes are choosing to do just that daily. Hebrews 10:26–27 declares, "If we deliberately keep on sinning after we have received the knowledge of the truth, no sacrifice for sins is left, but only the fearful expectation of judgment and of raging fire that will consume the enemies of God." A rejection of Christ is an acceptance of the responsibility to pay for your own sins. Accept the free gift of God and save your precious life.

Stop paying for your own sins and let Jesus treat you to heaven. Only perfection can satisfy justice, therefore all human effort will always fall short. The wages of sin is death, but the free gift of God is eternal life through Jesus Christ (Rom. 6:23). Accept His payment for your sin so you can focus on worship instead of work.

Prayer

Dear God, thank you for paying the price for my sin. I accept Your sacrifice and cease from my own efforts to prove my worthiness. I come before You to worship and let my work be an expression of my gratitude. In Jesus's name, amen.

DAY 16

Matthew 15:21–28

Then Jesus went out from there and departed to the region of Tyre and Sidon. And behold, a woman of Canaan came from that region and cried out to Him, saying, "Have mercy on me, O Lord, Son of David! My daughter is severely demon-possessed."

But He answered her not a word.

And His disciples came and urged Him, saying, "Send her away, for she cries out after us."

But He answered and said, "I was not sent except to the lost sheep of the house of Israel."

Then she came and worshiped Him, saying, "Lord, help me!"

But He answered and said, "It is not good to take the children's bread and throw *it* to the little dogs."

And she said, "Yes, Lord, yet even the little dogs eat the crumbs which fall from their masters' table."

Then Jesus answered and said to her, "O woman, great *is* your faith! Let it be to you as you desire." And her daughter was healed from that very hour.

DON'T STOP BELIEVING

Good day, Saints!

His silence threw me for a loop, but my daughter's agony kept my focus securely fixed nonetheless. In desperation, I cried out to His disciples, only to be confronted by their irritation. Then He spoke, and my heart sank. Everything inside of me wanted to run away and hide, but instead I found myself worshipping at His feet crying out, "Lord, help me!" His response to my plea was unexpected. My reaction was even more surprising. His final answer secured my daughter's healing and redefined my life. I will never forget His words, "O woman, great is your faith! Let it be to you as you desire" (Matt. 15:21–28).

Don't stop believing! Stand in the gap and allow for your faith in Jesus to anchor your soul. Our unshakable faith will engender divine intervention in the life of those around us. It will be tried and tested, but the final product will shine to the glory of God.

Prayer

Dear God, thank you for being so good to me. Help me to stay steadfast in you even when life doesn't make sense. Let my undaunted faith be a light of healing for those around me. In Jesus's name, amen.

2 Kings 13:10–19

In the thirty-seventh year of Joash king of Judah, Jehoash the son of Jehoahaz became king over Israel in Samaria, *and reigned* sixteen years. And he did evil in the sight of the Lord. He did not depart from all the sins of Jeroboam the son of Nebat, who made Israel sin, *but* walked in them.

Now the rest of the acts of Joash, all that he did, and his might with which he fought against Amaziah king of Judah, *are* they not written in the book of the chronicles of the kings of Israel? So Joash rested with his fathers. Then Jeroboam sat on his throne. And Joash was buried in Samaria with the kings of Israel.

Elisha had become sick with the illness of which he would die. Then Joash the king of Israel came down to him, and wept over his face, and said, "O my father, my father, the chariots of Israel and their horsemen!"

And Elisha said to him, "Take a bow and some arrows." So he took himself a bow and some arrows. Then he said to the king of Israel, "Put your hand on the bow." So he put his hand *on it,* and Elisha put his hands on the king's hands. And he said, "Open the east window"; and he opened *it.* Then Elisha said, "Shoot"; and he shot. And he said, "The arrow of the Lord's deliverance and the arrow of deliverance from Syria; for you must strike the Syrians at Aphek till you have destroyed *them.*" Then he said, "Take the arrows"; so he took *them.* And he said to the king of Israel, "Strike the ground"; so he struck three times, and stopped. And the man of God was angry with him, and said, "You should have struck five or six times; then you would have struck Syria till you had destroyed *it!* But now you will strike Syria *only* three times."

STRIKE THE GROUND

Good day, Saints!

After shooting the arrow out of the window, the prophet Elisha reassured King Jehoash that victory against his enemies was certain. Then the prophet instructed the king to take a handful of arrows and strike the ground. "Strike the ground? Why?" thought the king. He then haphazardly struck the ground three times. By contemning the sign, King Jehoash sealed his own demise. "If you would have struck the ground five or six times," said Elisha, "you would have completely destroyed your enemy, but now your victory will be short lived" (2 Kings 13:10–19).

Victory belongs to the Lord. Our gifts, talents, and resources can never provide security. Unwavering dependence on God's word is the only safe place we have. Therefore, lean wholeheartedly on Him. Strike the ground!

Prayer

Dear God, thank you for Your word. Help me to lean unwaveringly on Your word even when it doesn't make sense to me. Rid me of hubristic tendencies that blind my eyes to Your sovereignty. In Jesus's name, amen.

Psalms 126

When the Lord brought back the captivity of Zion,
We were like those who dream.
Then our mouth was filled with laughter,
And our tongue with singing.
Then they said among the nations,
"The Lord has done great things for them."
The Lord has done great things for us,
And we are glad.
Bring back our captivity, O Lord,
As the streams in the South.
Those who sow in tears
Shall reap in joy.
He who continually goes forth weeping,
Bearing seed for sowing,
Shall doubtless come again with rejoicing,
Bringing his sheaves *with him.*

DON'T STOP CRYING OUT

Good day, Saints!

The journey back home after years of captivity in the land of Babylon was filled with great joy and high expectation. We were witnessing the mighty hand of God moving miraculously in our midst. All the years of weeping before the Lord have paid off. Many times we were tempted to lose hope, but we knew that God was working all things out for our good. Those who sow in tears, will reap with songs of joy. He who goes out weeping, carrying seed to sow, will return with songs of joy carrying sheaves with him (Ps. 126:1–6).

Don't stop crying out! God is on the throne, and He hears our deepest heart's cry. Regardless of the ominous nature of the storm, God is still in control. Sow your seeds in faith. Weeping may endure for a night, but joy comes in the morning. Your harvest may not appear to be blossoming now, but in due season, you will enjoy the fruits of your labor. Get ready to shout for joy!

Prayer

Dear God, thank you for working all things out for my good. I know my season of harvest is coming, so I will continue to sow seeds of faith and practice my songs of joy in anticipation of Your blessings. In Jesus's name, amen.

Isaiah 54:1–4

"Sing, O barren, You *who* have not borne!
Break forth into singing, and cry aloud,
You *who* have not labored with child!
For more *are* the children of the desolate
Than the children of the married woman," says
the Lord.
"Enlarge the place of your tent,
And let them stretch out the curtains of your
dwellings;
Do not spare;
Lengthen your cords,
And strengthen your stakes.
For you shall expand to the right and to the left,
And your descendants will inherit the nations,
And make the desolate cities inhabited.
"Do not fear, for you will not be ashamed;
Neither be disgraced, for you will not be put to
shame;
For you will forget the shame of your youth,
And will not remember the reproach of your
widowhood anymore

ENLARGE YOUR TENT STAKES

Good day, Saints!
Say good-bye to the days of barrenness. Bid farewell to the years
of abandonment. Make room for increase. Don't hold back, build

bigger! You shall break forth in multiplication on the left and right. Your seed shall inherit the gentiles and make the desolate cities come alive again. Fear not! Shame will no longer call your name. The pain of your youth and the sorrows of widowhood will be remembered no more. For your Creator will be your Husband. God Almighty is His name. He is your Redeemer, the Holy God of Israel. The God of all the earth (Isa. 54:1–4).

Enlarge your tent stakes! Your redemption is near. The suffering servant will soon return as the glorious Bridegroom to receive His bride. Make room for Him in your heart. All the pain and sorrow of yesterday will be overshadowed by His unconditional love for you. Everything He has preordained for your life is about to manifest powerfully for His glory's sake. Hold nothing back. Get ready! This is the day the Lord has made for you. Enlarge your tent stakes!

Prayer

Dear God, thank you for supernatural increase. Let your blessings overtake me and wash away the shame of yesterday. Overflow into the dry places of my heart and make them come alive again. I make room for increase. In Jesus's name, amen.

Mark 9:1–41

And He said to them, "Assuredly, I say to you that there are some standing here who will not taste death till they see the kingdom of God present with power." Now after six days Jesus took Peter, James, and John, and led them up on a high mountain apart by themselves; and He was transfigured before them. His clothes became shining, exceedingly white, like snow, such as no launderer on earth can whiten them. And Elijah appeared to them with Moses, and they were talking with Jesus. Then Peter answered and said to Jesus, "Rabbi, it is good for us to be here; and let us make three tabernacles: one for You, one for Moses, and one for Elijah"—because he did not know what to say, for they were greatly afraid. And a cloud came and overshadowed them; and a voice came out of the cloud, saying, "This is My beloved Son. Hear Him!" Suddenly, when they had looked around, they saw no one anymore, but only Jesus with themselves. Now as they came down from the mountain, He commanded them that they should tell no one the things they had seen, till the Son of Man had risen from the dead. So they kept this word to themselves, questioning what the rising from the dead meant. And they asked Him, saying, "Why do the scribes say that Elijah must come first?" Then He answered and told them, "Indeed, Elijah is coming first and restores all things. And how is it written concerning the Son of Man, that He must suffer many things and be treated with contempt? But I say to you that Elijah has also come, and they did to him whatever they wished, as it is written of him." And when He came to the disciples, He saw a great multitude around them, and scribes disputing with them. Immediately, when they saw Him, all the people were greatly amazed, and running to Him, greeted Him. And He asked the scribes, "What are you discussing with them?" Then one of the crowd answered and said, "Teacher, I brought You my son, who has a mute spirit. And wherever it seizes him, it throws him down; he foams at the mouth, gnashes his teeth, and becomes rigid. So I spoke to Your disciples, that they should cast it out, but they could not." He answered him and said, "O faithless generation, how long shall I be with you? How long shall I bear with you? Bring him to Me." Then they brought him to Him. And when he saw Him, immediately the spirit convulsed him, and he fell on the ground and wallowed, foaming at the mouth. So He asked his father, "How long has this been happening to him?" And he said, "From childhood. And often he has thrown him both into the fire and into the water to destroy him. But if You can do anything, have compassion on us and help us." Jesus said to him, "If you can believe, all things are possible to him who believes." Immediately the father of the child cried out and said with tears, "Lord, I believe; help my unbelief!" When Jesus saw that the people came running together, He rebuked the unclean spirit, saying to it: "Deaf and dumb spirit, I command you, come out of him and enter him no more!" Then the spirit cried out, convulsed him greatly, and came out of him. And he became as one dead, so that many said, "He is dead." But Jesus took him by the hand and lifted him up, and he arose. And when He had come into the house, His disciples asked Him privately, "Why could we not cast it out?" So He said to them, "This kind can come out by nothing but prayer and fasting." Then they departed from there and passed through Galilee, and He did not want anyone to know it. For He taught His disciples and said to them, "The Son of Man is being betrayed into the hands of men, and they will kill Him. And after He is killed, He will rise the third day." But they did not understand this saying, and were afraid to ask Him. Then He came to Capernaum. And when He was in the house He asked them, "What was it you disputed among yourselves on the road?" But they kept silent, for on the road they had disputed among themselves who would be the greatest. And He sat down, called the twelve, and said to them, "If anyone desires to be first, he shall be last of all and servant of all." Then He took a little child and set him in the midst of them. And when He had taken him in His arms, He said to them, "Whoever receives one of these little children in My name receives Me; and whoever receives Me, receives not Me but Him who sent Me." Now John answered Him, saying, "Teacher, we saw someone who does not follow us casting out demons in Your name, and we forbade him because he does not follow us." But Jesus said, "Do not forbid him, for no one who works a miracle in My name can soon afterward speak evil of Me. For he who is not against us is on our side. For whoever gives you a cup of water to drink in My name, because you belong to Christ, assuredly, I say to you, he will by no means lose his reward.

PRINCIPLES TO GUIDE OUR WARFARE

Good day, Saints!

First John 3:8 declares, "For this purpose the Son of God was manifest, that He might destroy the works of the devil." Let us join Christ in the battle for the redemption of souls. Here are some basic principles to guide our warfare:

1. The power of the kingdom of God is not for the securing of health, wealth, or influence but for the breaking of demonic strongholds and setting people free to live a life of liberty in Jesus Christ. (Mark 9:1, 25–27, 38).
2. Recognize and submit to the deity of Christ (Mark 9:2–13).
3. All things are possible to him who believes (Mark 9:23).
4. Prayer and fasting weakens demonic strongholds (Mark 9:29).
5. Childlike faith increases spiritual authority (Mark 9:33–37).
6. In the name of Jesus Christ, we have authority to cast out demons and work miracles (Mark 9:38–40).
7. The power and blessing of the kingdom of God is accessible to everyone who believes (Mark 9:41).

Prayer

Dear God, thank you for preparing my hands for war. I recognize and submit to Your authority. Use me as a vessel to destroy the works of the devil and to be a light of hope for those in bondage. In Jesus's name, amen.

DAY 21

Mark 9:41

For whoever gives you a cup of water to drink in My name, because you belong to Christ, assuredly, I say to you, he will by no means lose his reward.

WATERBOYS ARE IMPORTANT TOO

Good day, Saints!

As the disciples argue over position and status, Jesus opens their understanding to the beauty resident in all things. "For whoever gives you a cup of water in My name because you belong to Christ," said Jesus. "Assuredly, I say to you, he will by no means lose his reward" (Mark 9:41). Blinded by the pursuit of recognition, the twelve were unable to see the gifts of God that surrounded them. If it didn't fit into their purview, then surely it was wrong. However, Christ elevates a seemingly mundane and insignificant act to the same level as a prophet and evangelist. They too shall receive their reward. Every person is important. Every person has something to give. When we see one another and the world around us in this light, our burden becomes lighter, our witness shines brighter, and our worship reverberates louder.

Take another look around you. What great blessing have you overlooked simply because it doesn't fit nicely into your comfort zone? Remember, waterboys will be honored in heaven too. Let's not take for granted the beauty God has placed all around us. Every person is important! Every person has something to give! Begin celebrating God's gifts!

Prayer

Dear God, thank you for all the beauty You have placed around me. Give me eyes that can see beyond my limitations so that I may boldly declare Your Word in the midst of doubt and unbelief. Help me to recognize and celebrate Your glory in every person and circumstance. In Jesus's name, amen.

Luke 2:8–22

Now there were in the same country shepherds living out in the fields, keeping watch over their flock by night. And behold, an angel of the Lord stood before them, and the glory of the Lord shone around them, and they were greatly afraid. Then the angel said to them, "Do not be afraid, for behold, I bring you good tidings of great joy which will be to all people. For there is born to you this day in the city of David a Savior, who is Christ the Lord. And this *will be* the sign to you: You will find a Babe wrapped in swaddling cloths, lying in a manger."

And suddenly there was with the angel a multitude of the heavenly host praising God and saying:
"Glory to God in the highest,
And on earth peace, goodwill toward men!"

So it was, when the angels had gone away from them into heaven, that the shepherds said to one another, "Let us now go to Bethlehem and see this thing that has come to pass, which the Lord has made known to us." And they came with haste and found Mary and Joseph, and the Babe lying in a manger. Now when they had seen *Him,* they made widely known the saying which was told them concerning this Child. And all those who heard *it* marveled at those things which were told them by the shepherds. But Mary kept all these things and pondered *them* in her heart. Then the shepherds returned, glorifying and praising God for all the things that they had heard and seen, as it was told them.

And when eight days were completed for the circumcision of the Child, His name was called Jesus, the name given by the angel before He was conceived in the womb.

Now when the days of her purification according to the law of Moses were completed, they brought Him to Jerusalem to present *Him* to the Lord.

Philippians 1:6

Being confident of this very thing, that He who has begun a good work in you will complete *it* until the day of Jesus Christ.

Romans 8:28

And we know that all things work together for good to those who love God, to those who are the called according to *His* purpose.

GOD WILL MEET YOU AT EVERY TURN

Good day, Saints!

It has been nine months since the angel gave me the news that has forever changed my life. How can it be that I, of all people would be chosen for such an awesome task? At every unexpected turn, God has faithfully settled my heart. Joseph's gracious understanding, my cousin Elizabeth's miracle baby and prophetic declaration, and now this much needed shelter during a very busy time in Bethlehem. I am nervously excited to fulfill my God given assignment, but I feel so woefully inadequate for the call. Later on that night, the shepherds who were watching their flock began lining up outside the manger, proclaiming, "For unto you is born this day in the city of David, a Savior, which is Christ the Lord" (Luke 2:8–22). Their message was exactly what my soul needed. Thank you, Lord! You know me through and through.

It is without question that your calling is much bigger than you are. Each step is more intimidating than the last, and quitting is a regular contemplation. However, He who began a good work in you is faithful to complete it (Phil.1:6). He knows what you need when you need it. God is diligently working to ensure the full manifestation of your destiny, therefore begin looking for His sovereign provision. Expect a miracle! Know that He is working all things out for the good of them that love God and are called according to His purpose (Rom. 8:28). He will meet you at every turn.

Prayer

Dear God, thank you for watching over me at every turn of my life. Even in the difficult times of uncertainty, I know You are holding my hand. Have Your way in me. In Jesus's name, amen.

Matthew 1:22–23

So all this was done that it might be fulfilled which was spoken by the Lord through the prophet, saying: "Behold, the virgin shall be with child, and bear a Son, and they shall call His name Immanuel," which is translated, "God with us."

Isaiah 7:14

Therefore the Lord Himself will give you a sign: Behold, the virgin shall conceive and bear a Son, and shall call His name Immanuel.

HIS WORD IS OUR ANCHOR

Good day, Saints!

When the supernatural overwhelms our natural sensibilities, God always directs our attention to the anchor of His word. His word gives the necessary parameter needed to discern the sometimes unpredictable nature of supernatural activity. Joseph was a devout and good man, but the news of his betrothed bride being with child by the Holy Spirit was too much to handle. Matthew 1:22–23, however, gives us insight into the process Joseph undertook to comprehend the genius of God. This was not a chance occurrence. Many years prior, God ordained this day through the word He gave the prophet Isaiah (Isa. 7:14). The angels were simply announcing what

God outlined from the beginning of time, and Joseph and Mary were given the blessing of participating with God in His divine plan of redemption. God's word confirmed the angel's message and that was all Joseph needed to fully embrace the joy and challenge of God's will.

God's plan for your life will always coincide with His word. Any direction received that is contrary to God's word, regardless if it is delivered by an angel, pastor, loved one, or self must be rejected. However, any direction from God will always remain consistent with His word and must be embraced even if it causes your faith to be stretched beyond your experience or comfort. It will perfect your character, increase your joy, and place you in the honorable position of being a co-laborer with Christ Jesus. God's will confirmed through God's word will keep us anchored as we follow God's way!

Prayer

Dear God, thank you for the anchor of Your word that settles my heart when my eyes are blurry. I humbly embrace Your will. In Jesus's name, amen.

Job 1:1–2:10

Now there was a day when his sons and daughters *were* eating and drinking wine in their oldest brother's house; and a messenger came to Job and said, "The oxen were plowing and the donkeys feeding beside them, when the Sabeans raided *them* and took them away—indeed they have killed the servants with the edge of the sword; and I alone have escaped to tell you!"

While he *was* still speaking, another also came and said, "The fire of God fell from heaven and burned up the sheep and the servants, and consumed them; and I alone have escaped to tell you!"

While he *was* still speaking, another also came and said, "The Chaldeans formed three bands, raided the camels and took them away, yes, and killed the servants with the edge of the sword; and I alone have escaped to tell you!"

While he *was* still speaking, another also came and said, "Your sons and daughters *were* eating and drinking wine in their oldest brother's house, and suddenly a great wind came from across the wilderness and struck the four corners of the house, and it fell on the young people, and they are dead; and I alone have escaped to tell you!"

Then Job arose, tore his robe, and shaved his head; and he fell to the ground and worshiped. And he said:

"Naked I came from my mother's womb,
And naked shall I return there.

The Lord gave, and the Lord has taken away;

Blessed be the name of the Lord."

In all this Job did not sin nor charge God with wrong.

Again there was a day when the sons of God came to present themselves before the Lord, and Satan came also among them to present himself before the Lord. And the Lord said to Satan, "From where do you come?"

Satan answered the Lord and said, "From going to and fro on the earth, and from walking back and forth on it."

Then the Lord said to Satan, "Have you considered My servant Job, that *there is* none like him on the earth, a blameless and upright man, one who fears God and shuns evil? And still he holds fast to his integrity, although you incited Me against him, to destroy him without cause."

So Satan answered the Lord and said, "Skin for skin! Yes, all that a man has he will give for his life. But stretch out Your hand now, and touch his bone and his flesh, and he will surely curse You to Your face!"

And the Lord said to Satan, "Behold, he *is* in your hand, but spare his life."

So Satan went out from the presence of the Lord, and struck Job with painful boils from the sole of his foot to the crown of his head. And he took for himself a potsherd with which to scrape himself while he sat in the midst of the ashes.

Then his wife said to him, "Do you still hold fast to your integrity? Curse God and die!"

But he said to her, "You speak as one of the foolish women speaks. Shall we indeed accept good from God, and shall we not accept adversity?" In all this Job did not sin with his lips.

MAKE THE DEVIL MAD

Good day, Saints!

He came waltzing in with the other angels after traversing the earth looking for something or someone to corrupt when God asked him, "Have you considered my servant Job? There is no one like him on earth, a perfect and upright man, one that fears God and shuns evil." Satan quickly retorted, "Does Job fear God for nothing? Remove your hand of protection and blessings from his life and he will curse You to Your face." From then on Satan began attacking Job relentlessly in order to discredit God's testimony of Job's unshakable godly character, but regardless of the merciless onslaught, Job never lost hope in the faithfulness of God. His unflinching trust in the goodness of God became a resounding indictment of Satan's unjustifiable rebellion against God. (Job 1:1–2,10)

A life fully surrendered to Jesus Christ glorifies God and makes the devil mad. Lucifer was unable to remain loyal to God in the midst of God's goodness, therefore he works incessantly to deceive humanity to follow his example. However, as you remain faithful to God and yield fully to His will, you will announce to the heavens how truly evil, prideful, self-absorbed, spineless, and foolish Satan is. Your pure worship of Jesus Christ in the crucible of mounting opposition against everything Christlike will send a message to the devil and his minions that their days are numbered.

Prayer

Dear God, thank you for enabling me to stand firm in the midst of the devil's attack on my faith in You. Make my life a living sacrifice, holy and acceptable unto You and indictment of evil. In the name of Jesus, amen.

Acts 27:39–28:10

When it was day, they did not recognize the land; but they observed a bay with a beach, onto which they planned to run the ship if possible. And they let go the anchors and left *them* in the sea, meanwhile loosing the rudder ropes; and they hoisted the mainsail to the wind and made for shore. But striking a place where two seas met, they ran the ship aground; and the prow stuck fast and remained immovable, but the stern was being broken up by the violence of the waves.

And the soldiers' plan was to kill the prisoners, lest any of them should swim away and escape. But the centurion, wanting to save Paul, kept them from *their* purpose, and commanded that those who could swim should jump *overboard* first and get to land, and the rest, some on boards and some on *parts* of the ship. And so it was that they all escaped safely to land.

Now when they had escaped, they then found out that the island was called Malta. And the natives showed us unusual kindness; for they kindled a fire and made us all welcome, because of the rain that was falling and because of the cold. But when Paul had gathered a bundle of sticks and laid *them* on the fire, a viper came out because of the heat, and fastened on his hand. So when the natives saw the creature hanging from his hand, they said to one another, "No doubt this man is a murderer, whom, though he has escaped the sea, yet justice does not allow to live." But he shook off the creature into the fire and suffered no harm. However, they were expecting that he would swell up or suddenly fall down dead. But after they had looked for a long time and saw no harm come to him, they changed their minds and said that he was a god.

In that region there was an estate of the leading citizen of the island, whose name was Publius, who received us and entertained us courteously for three days. And it happened that the father of Publius lay sick of a fever and dysentery. Paul went in to him and prayed, and he laid his hands on him and healed him. So when this was done, the rest of those on the island who had diseases also came and were healed. They also honored us in many ways; and when we departed, they provided such things as were necessary.

FROM BAD TO WORSE TO MIRACLES

Good day, Saints!

The ship they were in began breaking apart due to the violent winds and crashing waves. Fearing prisoners escaping, the soldiers planned to kill each one, but the centurion in charge intervened in order to save Paul's life. Everyone aboard the ship floated safely to shore and immediately began building a fire to keep themselves warm. As Paul warmed himself over the fire, a poisonous snake attached itself to his hand. The local residents were convinced that this man was a murderer because he escaped the violent sea but could not escape the viper's bite. In total amazement, they all watched as Paul simply shook the viper off into the fire and suffered no ill effects whatsoever. What followed was even more amazing. The sick and diseased throughout the whole island were healed and the gospel of Jesus Christ received (Acts 27:39–44, 28:1–10).

Miracles often begin in storms. Circumstances may go from bad to worse, but what is constant in the life of a follower of Jesus Christ is miracles. Every negative situation we encounter in life is an opportunity that God uses to save and heal those around us. It also serves as a reminder of God's complete commitment to the fulfillment of our destiny. If you find yourself coming out of a storm only to be bitten by a viper, take heart—miracles are about to begin.

Prayer

Dear God, thank you that You are not moved by adverse circumstances but will work all things out for my good and Your glory. Help me to remain steadfast when life appears to not make sense. In Jesus's name, amen.

DAY 26

Psalm 105:43–45

He brought out His people with joy,
His chosen ones with gladness.
He gave them the lands of the Gentiles,
And they inherited the labor of the nations,
That they might observe His statutes
And keep His laws.

BLESSED TO BE A BLESSING

Good day, Saints!

God brought His people out with joy and His chosen ones with gladness. He gave them the lands of the gentiles, and they inherited the labor of the nations, that they might observe His statutes and keep His laws. Years of bondage, forced labor, slavery, and oppression erased in one day. All barriers were removed and complete victory secured. The aimless life they once endured has been replaced by the privilege of living as shining lights of the glory of God. Nations who were ignorant of the grace of God now have the opportunity to know the Creator of the universe through the living witness of His people (Ps. 105:43–45).

We are blessed to be a blessing! Christ set us free from the bondage of sin and gave us a new lease on life. That new lease is not a license to indulge our selfish desires, but a responsibility to shine the light of God's love so our neighbors can discover the goodness of Jesus Christ. Be blessed. Live to bless.

Dear God, thank you for blessing me with victory from bondage. Help me to bless others as You have blessed me with Your love and truth. In Jesus's name, amen.

Acts 16:6–40

Now when they had gone through Phrygia and the region of Galatia, they were forbidden by the Holy Spirit to preach the word in Asia. After they had come to Mysia, they tried to go into Bithynia, but the Spirit did not permit them. So passing by Mysia, they came down to Troas. And a vision appeared to Paul in the night. A man of Macedonia stood and pleaded with him, saying, "Come over to Macedonia and help us." Now after he had seen the vision, immediately we sought to go to Macedonia, concluding that the Lord had called us to preach the gospel to them.

Therefore, sailing from Troas, we ran a straight course to Samothrace, and the next *day* came to Neapolis, and from there to Philippi, which is the foremost city of that part of Macedonia, a colony. And we were staying in that city for some days. And on the Sabbath day we went out of the city to the riverside, where prayer was customarily made; and we sat down and spoke to the women who met *there*. Now a certain woman named Lydia heard *us*. She was a seller of purple from the city of Thyatira, who worshiped God. The Lord opened her heart to heed the things spoken by Paul. And when she and her household were baptized, she begged *us*, saying, "If you have judged me to be faithful to the Lord, come to my house and stay." So she persuaded us.

Now it happened, as we went to prayer, that a certain slave girl possessed with a spirit of divination met us, who brought her masters much profit by fortune-telling. This girl followed Paul and us, and cried out, saying, "These men are the servants of the Most High God, who proclaim to us the way of salvation." And this she did for many days.

But Paul, greatly annoyed, turned and said to the spirit, "I command you in the name of Jesus Christ to come out of her." And he came out that very hour. But when her masters saw that their hope of profit was gone, they seized Paul and Silas and dragged *them* into the marketplace to the authorities.

And they brought them to the magistrates, and said, "These men, being Jews, exceedingly trouble our city; and they teach customs which are not lawful for us, being Romans, to receive or observe." Then the multitude rose up together against them; and the magistrates tore off their clothes and commanded *them* to be beaten with rods. And when they had laid many stripes on them, they threw *them* into prison, commanding the jailer to keep them securely. Having received such a charge, he put them into the inner prison and fastened their feet in the stocks.

But at midnight Paul and Silas were praying and singing hymns to God, and the prisoners were listening to them. Suddenly there was a great earthquake, so that the foundations of the prison were shaken; and immediately all the doors were opened and everyone's chains were loosed. And the keeper of the prison, awaking from sleep and seeing the prison doors open, supposing the prisoners had fled, drew his sword and was about to kill himself. But Paul called with a loud voice, saying, "Do yourself no harm, for we are all here."

Then he called for a light, ran in, and fell down trembling before Paul and Silas. And he brought them out and said, "Sirs, what must I do to be saved?"

So they said, "Believe on the Lord Jesus Christ, and you will be saved, you and your household." Then they spoke the word of the Lord to him and to all who were in his house. And he took them the same hour of the night and washed *their* stripes. And immediately he and all his *family* were baptized. Now when he had brought them into his house, he set food before them; and he rejoiced, having believed in God with all his household.

And when it was day, the magistrates sent the officers, saying, "Let those men go."

So the keeper of the prison reported these words to Paul, saying, "The magistrates have sent to let you go. Now therefore depart, and go in peace."

But Paul said to them, "They have beaten us openly, uncondemned Romans, *and* have thrown *us* into prison. And now do they put us out secretly? No indeed! Let them come themselves and get us out."

And the officers told these words to the magistrates, and they were afraid when they heard that they were Romans. Then they came and pleaded with them and brought *them* out, and asked *them* to depart from the city. So they went out of the prison and entered *the house of* Lydia; and when they had seen the brethren, they encouraged them and departed.

MY EYES ARE ON THE FAITHFUL

Good day, Saints!

Paul and Silas sought diligently to answer God's call to preach the gospel, but at each place they ventured into, the Holy Spirit forbade them to preach. This happened several times until one night Paul was shown a vision of a man from Macedonia bidding them to come over to help them. The dynamic duo knew immediately that this was the Lord's direction. As a result of their obedience, several miracles took place. A businesswoman by the name of Lydia, including her entire household, placed their faith in Christ Jesus. A young woman possessed by an evil spirit was set free from bondage, and a jailer, along with his family, committed their lives to Christ. What began as a series of closed doors became a lesson on time maximization. Miracles followed as they allowed the Lord to lead (Acts 16:6–40).

The eyes of the Lord are on the faithful. He sees all the closed doors. He is aware of the many disappointments. However, He also sees your faithful heart and is standing ready to open the right door that will trigger the maximization of your time and skill. As you stay diligent with the task at hand, He is preparing the next series of miracles designed specifically for your life. Keep your head up. God is watching!

Prayer

Dear God, thank you for watching out for me. When doors close in my face, I will rest in Your sovereign embrace knowing that You will make all things beautiful in Your time. In Jesus's name, amen.

DAY 28

Philippians 2:12–15

Therefore, my beloved, as you have always obeyed, not as in my presence only, but now much more in my absence, work out your own salvation with fear and trembling; for it is God who works in you both to will and to do for *His* good pleasure.

Do all things without complaining and disputing, that you may become blameless and harmless, children of God without fault in the midst of a crooked and perverse generation, among whom you shine as lights in the world.

Fear God So Others May Live

Good day, Saints!

You are the light of the world! Therefore, work out your salvation with fear and trembling. The witness of your life will provide a beacon of hope in a perverse and crooked generation. God will enable you to live intentionally. Accidents do not occur in the life of a disciple of Jesus Christ. Every step is perfectly orchestrated to maximize your shine. Walking upright is increasingly more difficult in our self-absorbed world, but God will lead and guide you so that your life may be a light that can guide others to Jesus (Phil.2:12–15).

You are more important to the success of those around you than you may think. Fear God, and live. Fear God, and others will live. A small candle lit in a dark room will illuminate enough light to allow those trapped within it to navigate an escape. Don't be blinded by the darkness. Shine your light—the freedom of many depends on it.

Prayer

Dear God, thank you for making me a light for the world to see. Empower me by Your Holy Spirit that I may stand so that others may be saved. In Jesus's name, amen.

Psalm 92:7–15

When the wicked spring up like grass,
And when all the workers of iniquity flourish,
It is that they may be destroyed forever.
But You, Lord, *are* on high forevermore.
For behold, Your enemies, O Lord,
For behold, Your enemies shall perish;
All the workers of iniquity shall be scattered.
But my horn You have exalted like a wild ox;
I have been anointed with fresh oil.
My eye also has seen *my desire* on my enemies;
My ears hear *my desire* on the wicked
Who rise up against me.
The righteous shall flourish like a palm tree,
He shall grow like a cedar in Lebanon.
Those who are planted in the house of the Lord
Shall flourish in the courts of our God.
They shall still bear fruit in old age;
They shall be fresh and flourishing,
To declare that the Lord is upright;
He is my rock, and *there is* no unrighteousness in
Him.

DON'T BE INTIMIDATED

Good day, Saints!

The wicked flourish, and the evildoer will blossom with success;
but their life span is like that of a weed, and their destiny is eternal

destruction. In contrast, the godly will flourish like palm trees and grow strong like the cedars of Lebanon. Because they are planted in the house of the Lord, they will flourish in the courts of our God. They will consistently be producing fruit even as their hair turns gray. Their life will testify of the justice, faithfulness, and goodness of God (Ps. 92:7–15).

Don't be intimidated by the arrogance of the wicked. Their glory will be short-lived. Run into the house of God. Enter His courts with praise. Draw the line. Take your stand. Make Jesus the sole object of your pursuit. Drown out the drumbeat of despair with the unfailing song of God's everlasting goodness and faithfulness. You were born for such a time as this.

Prayer

Dear God, thank you for giving me the courage to stand on Your truth. Help me not to be intimidated by the increasing allure of sin. In Jesus's name, amen.

Matthew 6:10

Your kingdom come.
Your will be done
On earth as *it is* in heaven

Isaiah 62:1–12

For Zion's sake I will not hold My peace,
And for Jerusalem's sake I will not rest,
Until her righteousness goes forth as brightness,
And her salvation as a lamp *that* burns.
The Gentiles shall see your righteousness,
And all kings your glory.
You shall be called by a new name,
Which the mouth of the Lord will name.
You shall also be a crown of glory
In the hand of the Lord,
And a royal diadem
In the hand of your God.
You shall no longer be termed Forsaken,
Nor shall your land any more be termed Desolate;
But you shall be called Hephzibah, and your land
Beulah;
For the Lord delights in you,
And your land shall be married.
For *as* a young man marries a virgin,
So shall your sons marry you;
And *as* the bridegroom rejoices over the bride,
So shall your God rejoice over you.
I have set watchmen on your walls, O Jerusalem;

They shall never hold their peace day or night.
You who make mention of the Lord, do not keep
silent,
And give Him no rest till He establishes
And till He makes Jerusalem a praise in the earth.
The Lord has sworn by His right hand
And by the arm of His strength:
"Surely I will no longer give your grain
As food for your enemies;
And the sons of the foreigner shall not drink your
new wine,
For which you have labored.
But those who have gathered it shall eat it,
And praise the Lord;
Those who have brought it together shall drink it
in My holy courts."
Go through,
Go through the gates!
Prepare the way for the people;
Build up,
Build up the highway!
Take out the stones,
Lift up a banner for the peoples!
Indeed the Lord has proclaimed
To the end of the world:
"Say to the daughter of Zion,
'Surely your salvation is coming;
Behold, His reward *is* with Him,
And His work before Him.'"
And they shall call them The Holy People,
The Redeemed of the Lord;
And you shall be called Sought Out,
A City Not Forsaken.

WATCHMEN, ARISE

Good day, Saints!

In Matthew 6:10, Jesus taught His disciples to pray, "Thy kingdom come, Thy will be done in earth as it is in heaven." God speaking through the prophet Isaiah said, "I have set watchmen upon thy walls, O Jerusalem, which shall never hold their peace day or night. Ye that make mention of the Lord, keep not silence, and give Him no rest till He establish and till He makes Jerusalem a praise in the earth." Watchmen, arise and declare that what God's people have sown will no longer be pillaged. The wine produced in their vineyards will be enjoyed in the courts of their God. Go through and prepare the way for the people. Build up a highway and remove the stones. Lift up a standard for the people. Remind them that their salvation is nearer now than when they first believed. Christ is coming back soon for His bride. He will not allow her to be ravaged by her enemies. He is her defender. He will fight to keep her pure and unblemished. She will shine with the brightness of holiness and her lamp will not fail (Isa. 62:1–12).

Watchmen! Arise! Prepare the bride of Christ. Strengthen her hands for worship. Encourage her heart to believe the promises of God. Prepare the way so she can run unhindered by the enemies of God. Remind her of her identity. She is the bride of Christ. Her bridegroom sees and knows, and He will not disappoint. Watchmen, give yourselves no rest until she is properly prepared for her big day.

Prayer

Dear God, thank you for calling me to be a watchman on the wall. Help me to use the gifts and voice You have given me to prepare Your people for You. In the name of Jesus, amen.

Judges 6:1–14

Then the children of Israel did evil in the sight of the Lord. So the Lord delivered them into the hand of Midian for seven years, and the hand of Midian prevailed against Israel. Because of the Midianites, the children of Israel made for themselves the dens, the caves, and the strongholds which *are* in the mountains. So it was, whenever Israel had sown, Midianites would come up; also Amalekites and the people of the East would come up against them. Then they would encamp against them and destroy the produce of the earth as far as Gaza, and leave no sustenance for Israel, neither sheep nor ox nor donkey. For they would come up with their livestock and their tents, coming in as numerous as locusts; both they and their camels were without number; and they would enter the land to destroy it. So Israel was greatly impoverished because of the Midianites, and the children of Israel cried out to the Lord.

And it came to pass, when the children of Israel cried out to the Lord because of the Midianites, that the Lord sent a prophet to the children of Israel, who said to them, "Thus says the Lord God of Israel: 'I brought you up from Egypt and brought you out of the house of bondage; and I delivered you out of the hand of the Egyptians and out of the hand of all who oppressed you, and drove them out before you and gave you their land. Also I said to you, "I *am* the Lord your God; do not fear the gods of the Amorites, in whose land you dwell." But you have not obeyed My voice.'"

Now the Angel of the Lord came and sat under the terebinth tree which *was* in Ophrah, which *belonged* to Joash the Abiezrite, while his son Gideon threshed wheat in the winepress, in order to hide *it* from the Midianites. And the Angel of the Lord appeared to him, and said to him, "The Lord *is* with you, you mighty man of valor!"

Gideon said to Him, "O my lord, if the Lord is with us, why then has all this happened to us? And where *are* all His miracles which our fathers told us about, saying, 'Did not the Lord bring us up from Egypt?' But now the Lord has forsaken us and delivered us into the hands of the Midianites."

Then the Lord turned to him and said, "Go in this might of yours, and you shall save Israel from the hand of the Midianites. Have I not sent you?"

KEEP THRESHING THE WHEAT

Good day, Saints!

It's been seven long years, and still I find myself hiding in this winepress threshing wheat. When will this nightmare end? Where are the miracles our forefathers sang about? How long must we suffer under these deplorable circumstances? Does God not see our plight? As Gideon went about his daily routine, God unexpectedly appeared and commended him on his tenacious faith. "You are a mighty man of valor," said the Lord, "Go in this your strength and save your peo-

76

ple from their enemies." For seven years, you have faithfully stood in the gap. You fought through the temptations to quit, endured the many dark and lonely nights of the unknown, and never stopped believing for a miracle. You are a mighty man of God (Judg. 6:1–14).

Keep threshing the wheat! Fight through the discouragements. Look beyond the disappointments. Fix your eyes on the Author and Finisher of the faith. When you least expect it, He will show up and provide the necessary strength to complete the task. Keep threshing the wheat!

Prayer

Dear God, thank you for remembering my service unto You. With Your power, I will fight the good fight of faith. In Jesus's name, amen.

John 21:15–22

So when they had eaten breakfast, Jesus said to Simon Peter, "Simon, *son* of Jonah, do you love Me more than these?"

He said to Him, "Yes, Lord; You know that I love You."

He said to him, "Feed My lambs."

He said to him again a second time, "Simon, *son* of Jonah, do you love Me?"

He said to Him, "Yes, Lord; You know that I love You."

He said to him, "Tend My sheep."

He said to him the third time, "Simon, *son* of Jonah, do you love Me?" Peter was grieved because He said to him the third time, "Do you love Me?"

And he said to Him, "Lord, You know all things; You know that I love You."

Jesus said to him, "Feed My sheep. Most assuredly, I say to you, when you were younger, you girded yourself and walked where you wished; but when you are old, you will stretch out your hands, and another will gird you and carry *you* where you do not wish." This He spoke, signifying by what death he would glorify God. And when He had spoken this, He said to him, "Follow Me."

Then Peter, turning around, saw the disciple whom Jesus loved following, who also had leaned on His breast at the supper, and said, "Lord, who is the one who betrays You?" Peter, seeing him, said to Jesus, "But Lord, what *about* this man?"

Jesus said to him, "If I will that he remain till I come, what *is that* to you? You follow Me."

YOU FOLLOW ME

Good day, Saints!

After the third time of reaffirming his love for Jesus, Peter would be given a glimpse into his future. Christ revealed to him the kind of suffering he would endure, and the painful way he would die for the sake of the gospel. The next command Jesus gives Peter is shocking in light of the previous revelation, "Follow me." Peter, in his usual fashion, retorted, "What about him?" He was referring to John. Jesus answered, "If I will that he tarry 'til I come, what is that to you? You follow me." In other words, what I do with him is none of your business. Your responsibility is to follow me (John 21:15–22).

Following Jesus is not for the weak of heart. It will demand your best. Christ is calling us to complete surrender to His will. The days of comparing ourselves with one another must stop. We all have a specific task that we have been entrusted with. The details will differ, but our obedience to follow Jesus will nonetheless result in great glory and honor to God.

Prayer

Dear God, thank you for the invitation to follow You and the unique details You have ordained for my life. Help me to keep my eyes on You. In Jesus's name, amen.

Isaiah 40:27–31

Why do you say, O Jacob,
And speak, O Israel:
"My way is hidden from the Lord,
And my just claim is passed over by my God"?
Have you not known?
Have you not heard?
The everlasting God, the Lord,
The Creator of the ends of the earth,
Neither faints nor is weary.
His understanding is unsearchable.
He gives power to the weak,
And to *those who have* no might He increases strength.
Even the youths shall faint and be weary,
And the young men shall utterly fall,
But those who wait on the Lord
Shall renew *their* strength;
They shall mount up with wings like eagles,
They shall run and not be weary,
They shall walk and not faint.

GET READY TO SOAR

Good day, Saints!

"God has forgotten about our needs" and "God doesn't see the injustice we've been enduring" were sentiments expressed by Israel to God. Days, weeks, months, and years of uncertainty have passed by, and yet God is seemingly absent from the stage. Has He grown indifferent toward us? Nothing could be more distant from the truth. God answers, "Have you not known? Have you not heard? The everlasting God the Lord, the creator of the ends of the earth neither faints nor is weary. His understanding is unsearchable. He gives power to the weak, and to those who have no might. He increases strength. Even the youth shall faint and be weary, and the young men shall utterly fall, but those who wait on the Lord shall renew their strength. They shall mount up with wings like eagles, they shall run and not be weary, and they shall walk and not faint" (Isa. 40:27–31).

God is never negligent concerning anything especially in regards to His children. He broods over us with a Father's love, compassion, and protection. He has been working overtime to prepare every detail pertaining to our inheritance. Therefore, get ready. Be expectant. Stand in faith. At any moment He is going to cause us to mount up with wings as eagles and soar above it all.

Prayer

Dear God, thank you for being near to me even when I am in doubt. I stand ready by Your Spirit to soar above it all. In the name of Jesus, amen.

John 6:1–14

After these things Jesus went over the Sea of Galilee, which is *the Sea* of Tiberias. Then a great multitude followed Him, because they saw His signs which He performed on those who were diseased. And Jesus went up on the mountain, and there He sat with His disciples.

Now the Passover, a feast of the Jews, was near. Then Jesus lifted up *His* eyes, and seeing a great multitude coming toward Him, He said to Philip, "Where shall we buy bread, that these may eat?" But this He said to test him, for He Himself knew what He would do.

Philip answered Him, "Two hundred denarii worth of bread is not sufficient for them, that every one of them may have a little."

One of His disciples, Andrew, Simon Peter's brother, said to Him, "There is a lad here who has five barley loaves and two small fish, but what are they among so many?"

Then Jesus said, "Make the people sit down." Now there was much grass in the place. So the men sat down, in number about five thousand. And Jesus took the loaves, and when He had given thanks He distributed *them* to the disciples, and the disciples to those sitting down; and likewise of the fish, as much as they wanted. So when they were filled, He said to His disciples, "Gather up the fragments that remain, so that nothing is lost." Therefore they gathered *them* up, and filled twelve baskets with the fragments of the five barley loaves which were left over by those who had eaten. Then those men, when they had seen the sign that Jesus did, said, "This is truly the Prophet who is to come into the world."

WHAT YOU HAVE IS MORE THAN ENOUGH

Good day, Saints!

His answer revealed more than the facts concerning the crowd. It gives us insight into the perspective the disciples had of themselves and Jesus Christ. Andrew, Simon Peter's brother, said to Jesus, "There is a lad here who has five barley loaves and two fishes, but what are they among so many?" (John 6:8–9). This reaction is reminiscent of the children of Israel complaining in the wilderness after being freed from four hundred years of slavery in Egypt. They were so accustomed to being oppressed that they failed to see that all Jesus needed to perform a miracle was already in their hands. Jesus took the five barley loaves and two fishes from Andrew and fed five thousand men and their families. Then He gave each disciple a basket full of fish and bread for their personal enjoyment. The disciples discovered that day that what they had was more than enough to meet any challenge, as long as it was placed in God's hands (John 6:1–14).

Prayer

Thank you, God, for all that You have given us. We speak blessings over it and publicly announce that it is more than enough to meet every challenge. We place all we have in Your mighty hands. We declare that every provision for the vision You have entrusted to us will manifest fully because with You we have more than enough. In the name of Jesus, amen.

John 4:1–30

Therefore, when the Lord knew that the Pharisees had heard that Jesus made and baptized more disciples than John (though Jesus Himself did not baptize, but His disciples), He left Judea and departed again to Galilee. But He needed to go through Samaria.

So He came to a city of Samaria which is called Sychar, near the plot of ground that Jacob gave to his son Joseph. Now Jacob's well was there. Jesus therefore, being wearied from *His* journey, sat thus by the well. It was about the sixth hour.

A woman of Samaria came to draw water. Jesus said to her, "Give Me a drink." For His disciples had gone away into the city to buy food.

Then the woman of Samaria said to Him, "How is it that You, being a Jew, ask a drink from me, a Samaritan woman?" For Jews have no dealings with Samaritans.

Jesus answered and said to her, "If you knew the gift of God, and who it is who says to you, 'Give Me a drink,' you would have asked Him, and He would have given you living water."

The woman said to Him, "Sir, You have nothing to draw with, and the well is deep. Where then do You get that living water? Are You greater than our father Jacob, who gave us the well, and drank from it himself, as well as his sons and his livestock?"

Jesus answered and said to her, "Whoever drinks of this water will thirst again, but whoever drinks of the water that I shall give him will never thirst. But the water that I shall give him will become in him a fountain of water springing up into everlasting life."

The woman said to Him, "Sir, give me this water, that I may not thirst, nor come here to draw."

Jesus said to her, "Go, call your husband, and come here."

The woman answered and said, "I have no husband."

Jesus said to her, "You have well said, 'I have no husband,' for you have had five husbands, and the one whom you now have is not your husband; in that you spoke truly."

The woman said to Him, "Sir, I perceive that You are a prophet. Our fathers worshiped on this mountain, and you *Jews* say that in Jerusalem is the place where one ought to worship."

Jesus said to her, "Woman, believe Me, the hour is coming when you will neither on this mountain, nor in Jerusalem, worship the Father. You worship what you do not know; we know what we worship, for salvation is of the Jews. But the hour is coming, and now is, when the true worshipers will worship the Father in spirit and truth; for the Father is seeking such to worship Him. God *is* Spirit, and those who worship Him must worship in spirit and truth."

The woman said to Him, "I know that Messiah is coming" (who is called Christ). "When He comes, He will tell us all things."

Jesus said to her, "I who speak to you am *He*."

And at this *point* His disciples came, and they marveled that He talked with a woman; yet

85

no one said, "What do You seek?" or, "Why are You talking with her?"

The woman then left her waterpot, went her way into the city, and said to the men, "Come, see a Man who told me all things that I ever did. Could this be the Christ?" Then they went out of the city and came to Him.

KICK THE BUCKET

Good day, Saints!

Her routine was predictable. Wait for the other women to leave, then fill up the bucket and continue on with the day. On this particular day, however, all of that would change. As she approached Jacob's well to retrieve some water, Jesus invited her to drink from the well of living water. Her hesitation to Christ's invitation revealed the depth of her pain. Immediately, Jesus began peeling away the layers of religiosity, shame, and fear that restricted her from receiving love. Once the barriers were removed, she was able to recognize that Jesus was the Messiah. Without delay, she left her waterpot and began announcing to her city the greatness of the new Man in her life (John 4:1–30).

Kick the bucket! Stop the madness! There is a better way. Shame and fear, regardless of how we camouflage them, will always blind us to God's best. Jesus is inviting us to commune with Him. Kick the bucket and let Jesus be the reason for our life.

Prayer

Dear God, thank you for the drink of new life You have given me. Peel away all the layers of shame and fear that are blinding my eyes from Your goodness. In the name of Jesus, amen.

John 2:1–11

On the third day there was a wedding in Cana of Galilee, and the mother of Jesus was there. Now both Jesus and His disciples were invited to the wedding. And when they ran out of wine, the mother of Jesus said to Him, "They have no wine."

Jesus said to her, "Woman, what does your concern have to do with Me? My hour has not yet come."

His mother said to the servants, "Whatever He says to you, do *it*."

Now there were set there six waterpots of stone, according to the manner of purification of the Jews, containing twenty or thirty gallons apiece. Jesus said to them, "Fill the waterpots with water." And they filled them up to the brim. And He said to them, "Draw *some* out now, and take *it* to the master of the feast." And they took *it*. When the master of the feast had tasted the water that was made wine, and did not know where it came from (but the servants who had drawn the water knew), the master of the feast called the bridegroom. And he said to him, "Every man at the beginning sets out the good wine, and when the *guests* have well drunk, then the inferior. You have kept the good wine until now!"

This beginning of signs Jesus did in Cana of Galilee, and manifested His glory; and His disciples believed in Him.

FILL UP THE BUCKETS

Good day, Saints!

"They're out of wine," said Mary to Jesus. Then she instructed the servants, saying, "Whatever He says to you, do it." Jesus immediately directed the servants to fill up the six stone waterpots used for ceremonial cleansing to the brim with water. Each waterpot was twenty to thirty gallons in size. After the waterpots were filled, Jesus ordered the servants to give the first cup to the governor of the feast. "Wow!" shouted the governor. "This is good wine." He called forth the bridegroom and commended him saying, "You have saved the best for last" (John 2:1–11).

The celebration is already in progress, and one of the most important ingredients of the feast has run out. What do we do now? The answer is simple. Pray, listen, and obey. Jesus was concerned about the success of this wedding feast, and He is also concerned about the success of your life. Whatever He tells you to do, do it. Your obedience will bring glory to the Bridegroom and success to your life. Go ahead and fill up the buckets!

Prayer

Dear God, thank you for being concerned about the success of my life. I yield to Your direction and wisdom. In the name of Jesus, amen.

Luke 24:13–35

Now behold, two of them were traveling that same day to a village called Emmaus, which was seven miles from Jerusalem. And they talked together of all these things which had happened. So it was, while they conversed and reasoned, that Jesus Himself drew near and went with them. But their eyes were restrained, so that they did not know Him.

And He said to them, "What kind of conversation *is* this that you have with one another as you walk and are sad?"

Then the one whose name was Cleopas answered and said to Him, "Are You the only stranger in Jerusalem, and have You not known the things which happened there in these days?"

And He said to them, "What things?"

So they said to Him, "The things concerning Jesus of Nazareth, who was a Prophet mighty in deed and word before God and all the people, and how the chief priests and our rulers delivered Him to be condemned to death, and crucified Him. But we were hoping that it was He who was going to redeem Israel. Indeed, besides all this, today is the third day since these things happened. Yes, and certain women of our company, who arrived at the tomb early, astonished us. When they did not find His body, they came saying that they had also seen a vision of angels who said He was alive. And certain of those *who were* with us went to the tomb and found *it* just as the women had said; but Him they did not see."

Then He said to them, "O foolish ones, and slow of heart to believe in all that the prophets have spoken! Ought not the Christ to have suffered these things and to enter into His glory?" And beginning at Moses and all the Prophets, He expounded to them in all the Scriptures the things concerning Himself.

Then they drew near to the village where they were going, and He indicated that He would have gone farther. But they constrained Him, saying, "Abide with us, for it is toward evening, and the day is far spent." And He went in to stay with them.

Now it came to pass, as He sat at the table with them, that He took bread, blessed and broke *it,* and gave it to them. Then their eyes were opened and they knew Him; and He vanished from their sight.

And they said to one another, "Did not our heart burn within us while He talked with us on the road, and while He opened the Scriptures to us?" So they rose up that very hour and returned to Jerusalem, and found the eleven and those *who were* with them gathered together, saying, "The Lord is risen indeed, and has appeared to Simon!" And they told about the things *that had happened* on the road, and how He was known to them in the breaking of bread.

WHEN YOU LEAST EXPECT IT

Good day, Saints!

Sadness and disappointment filled the air. They were expecting a political and military Messiah to restore the glory of Israel, but now their hope was dead. To make matters worse, a rumor has been spreading that the tomb where the body of Jesus lay is empty. In frustration, two disciples decide to leave Jerusalem and walk back home to Emmaus. As they travel along the road discussing the weekend's events, Jesus drew near and began walking with them. When He broke bread and began serving them, their eyes were suddenly opened and they recognized it was Jesus. They immediately returned to Jerusalem and joyously shared with the eleven all that Christ revealed. (Luke 24:13–35).

When it appears that nothing is moving in the direction you were hoping for, and faith is fading fast, look up! When you least expect it, Jesus will reveal His plan and purpose to you. He will make sense of the seemingly disconnected details and bring you back to that place of communion with Himself that will set the proper perspective for the rest of your life. He will not leave you in the dark. When you least expect it, the light will shine through.

Prayer

Dear God, thank you for making sense of the details in my life. Help me to recognize Your grace when life doesn't make sense. In the name of Jesus, amen.

Revelation 3:7–13

And to the angel of the church in Philadelphia write,
"These things says He who is holy, He who is true, 'He who has the key of David, He who opens and no one shuts, and shuts and no one opens': 'I know your works. See, I have set before you an open door, and no one can shut it; for you have a little strength, have kept My word, and have not denied My name. Indeed I will make *those* of the synagogue of Satan, who say they are Jews and are not, but lie—indeed I will make them come and worship before your feet, and to know that I have loved you. Because you have kept My command to persevere, I also will keep you from the hour of trial which shall come upon the whole world, to test those who dwell on the earth. Behold, I am coming quickly! Hold fast what you have, that no one may take your crown. He who overcomes, I will make him a pillar in the temple of My God, and he shall go out no more. I will write on him the name of My God and the name of the city of My God, the New Jerusalem, which comes down out of heaven from My God. And *I will write on him* My new name.
'He who has an ear, let him hear what the Spirit says to the churches.'"

STAY IN THE RACE

Good day, Saints!

They were surrounded by competing voices, locked out of places of worship, and nearly depleted in strength, but they continued to acknowledge God's name, and keep God's word. Their commitment to perseverance invited the protection of God from the hour of temptation that was coming on the whole world. A place of security was also reserved for them in the temple of God, and they would forever be recognized by a new name. All they needed to do was stay in the race. Jesus told them to hold on to what they had lest someone take their crown. Philadelphia was a city familiar with sports activity, so this message rang loud and clear to the whole world (Rev. 3:7–13).

Fight the temptation to give up. This too shall pass. In our weakness, His strength is made perfect. Stand on God's word and declare His name. He who began a good work in you is faithful to complete it. Stay in the race!

Prayer

Dear God, thank you for the encouragement of Your protection and presence in the midst of my walk of faith. I will continue to declare Your word and acknowledge Your name. In the name of Jesus, amen.

Luke 16:1–13

He also said to His disciples: "There was a certain rich man who had a steward, and an accusation was brought to him that this man was wasting his goods. So he called him and said to him, 'What is this I hear about you? Give an account of your stewardship, for you can no longer be steward.'

"Then the steward said within himself, 'What shall I do? For my master is taking the stewardship away from me. I cannot dig; I am ashamed to beg. I have resolved what to do, that when I am put out of the stewardship, they may receive me into their houses.'

"So he called every one of his master's debtors to *him,* and said to the first, 'How much do you owe my master?' And he said, 'A hundred measures of oil.' So he said to him, 'Take your bill, and sit down quickly and write fifty.' Then he said to another, 'And how much do you owe?' So he said, 'A hundred measures of wheat.' And he said to him, 'Take your bill, and write eighty.' So the master commended the unjust steward because he had dealt shrewdly. For the sons of this world are more shrewd in their generation than the sons of light.

"And I say to you, make friends for yourselves by unrighteous mammon, that when you fail, they may receive you into an everlasting home. He who *is* faithful in *what is* least is faithful also in much; and he who is unjust in *what is* least is unjust also in much. Therefore if you have not been faithful in the unrighteous mammon, who will commit to your trust the true *riches?* And if you have not been faithful in what is another man's, who will give you what is your own?

"No servant can serve two masters; for either he will hate the one and love the other, or else he will be loyal to the one and despise the other. You cannot serve God and mammon."

Romans 2:4

Or do you despise the riches of His goodness, forbearance, and longsuffering, not knowing that the goodness of God leads you to repentance?

GRACE ATTRACTS GRACE

Good day, Saints!

He was guilty as charged, but digging ditches or begging for money was completely out of the question. So the unfaithful manager decided to use a tactic that he neglected to employ beforehand called "grace relations." Everyone that owed a debt to his boss was contacted and informed that half or a significant amount of their debt was being forgiven. The news of his efforts quickly reached the landowner and the entire temper of their relationship changed. Instead of condemnation he was now being commended. His actions declared to the world that the landowner was kind and benevolent. It also accentuates the importance of using our wealth, position, or influence to serve others (Luke 16:1–13).

Grace attracts grace. It's the kindness of God that leads people to repentance (Rom. 2:4). As we apply grace in our day-to-day interactions with others, it allows the Spirit of grace to draw them into the loving arms of the Father. Nothing reflects the love of God better to a world in debt than God's people abounding in grace.

Prayer

Dear God, thank you for being so gracious to me even though I don't deserve it. Help me to be gracious to others that I may be Your reflection in a hurting world. In the name of Jesus, amen.

Revelation 1:9–20

I, John, both your brother and companion in the tribulation and kingdom and patience of Jesus Christ, was on the island that is called Patmos for the word of God and for the testimony of Jesus Christ. I was in the Spirit on the Lord's Day, and I heard behind me a loud voice, as of a trumpet, saying, "I am the Alpha and the Omega, the First and the Last," and, "What you see, write in a book and send *it* to the seven churches which are in Asia: to Ephesus, to Smyrna, to Pergamos, to Thyatira, to Sardis, to Philadelphia, and to Laodicea."

Then I turned to see the voice that spoke with me. And having turned I saw seven golden lampstands, and in the midst of the seven lampstands *One* like the Son of Man, clothed with a garment down to the feet and girded about the chest with a golden band. His head and hair *were* white like wool, as white as snow, and His eyes like a flame of fire; His feet *were* like fine brass, as if refined in a furnace, and His voice as the sound of many waters; He had in His right hand seven stars, out of His mouth went a sharp two-edged sword, and His countenance *was* like the sun shining in its strength. And when I saw Him, I fell at His feet as dead. But He laid His right hand on me, saying to me, "Do not be afraid; I am the First and the Last. I *am* He who lives, and was dead, and behold, I am alive forevermore. Amen. And I have the keys of Hades and of Death. Write the things which you have seen, and the things which are, and the things which will take place after this. The mystery of the seven stars which you saw in My right hand, and the seven golden lampstands: The seven stars are the angels of the seven churches, and the seven lampstands which you saw are the seven churches."

KEEP YOUR EYES ON JESUS

Good day, Saints!

In the heat of social, political, and economic persecution, the apostle John encourages the suffering church to keep their eyes on Jesus. The description he gives of Jesus would be vastly different than the Lamb of God that many of them saw slain on the cross. John announces the revelation of the Lion of Judah, who is the mighty Son of God. He has wooly white hair representing wisdom and divinity. Fiery eyes to bring judgment upon all evil. A golden band around His chest confirming His work as High Priest. Bronze feet signifying His kingship. And a sword in His mouth emphasizing the force and power of His message. He is identified as "First and Last," reiterating that victory was secure. Christ announces that He holds the keys of hell and death, which serves as a reminder to the saints that all authority has been given to Him. Regardless of the outward appearance, Jesus will have the last say (Rev. 1:9–20).

What do we do when it appears that evil is gaining the upper hand? Where do we turn when persecution shows up on our door step? The answer is just as true today as it was in John's day: "Keep your eyes on Jesus." He is the first and last; therefore victory is secure. So regardless of how loud evil roars in your life, just remember that Jesus will have the last word.

Prayer

Dear God, thank you for a fresh revelation of Jesus as the Lion of the tribe of Judah. Help me to keep my eyes focused on You regardless of the external pressures. In Jesus's name, amen.

ABOUT THE AUTHOR

Pana Mamea is a husband and father of three. He is the lead pastor of Hilltop Christian Center, an inner-city church in Tacoma, Washington, where he has served for the past twenty-plus years. Producing strong disciples and mobilizing the Body of Christ is his passion. God has enabled him to mobilize thousands of short- and long-term missionaries into twenty-five nations, as well as aid in the planting of twenty-plus churches. "Rebuilding broken dreams" is his life's motto. He believes that every individual has a God-ordained plan for their life, and regardless of the challenges life brings, a relationship with Jesus Christ will realign and propel it forward.

CPSIA information can be obtained
at www.ICGtesting.com
Printed in the USA
BVHW071226220221
600770BV00005B/399